STUDIES IN MODERN EUROPEAN LITERATURE AND THOUGHT

General Editor:
ERICH HELLER
Professor of German
in the University College of Swansea

UNAMUNO

Also published in this Series:

Roy Campbell: LORCA
Hans Egon Holthusen: RILKE
P. Mansell Jones: BAUDELAIRE
L. S. Salzberger: HÖLDERLIN
Elizabeth Sewell: PAUL VALÉRY
Cecil Sprigge: BENEDETTO CROCE

Other titles are in preparation

UNAMUNO

BY

ARTURO BAREA

NEW HAVEN
YALE UNIVERSITY PRESS
1952

Printed in the United States of America

This essay was written in collaboration with my wife,
Ilsa Barea, who also translated it

I

Unamuno and the National Problem

From time to time, men arise who embody the qualities, the mood or the ambitions of their peoples so forcibly that they achieve an extraordinary influence, a symbolic greatness, which belong to their persons rather than to their achievements. We have known some such men in our time, nearly all of them in the political sphere. It is a much rarer thing for a writer to become the acknowledged incarnation of the spirit of his people, for the scope of his work is by its very nature more limited than that of public action. He may, however, grow to universal significance through exploring his own mind, and the mind of the nation with which he finds himself identified. This is, I think, the case with the Spaniard Miguel de Unamuno.

It would be pointless to classify Unamuno in conventional terms. He was a thinker, essayist, novelist, poet, playwright and prolific journalist; he was a university professor, a deputy to the Spanish Cortes, and a self-appointed prophet. A great writer or philosopher? Not one of his creative works is completely satisfying as a work of art; not one of his essays expresses a consistent original philosophy. A leader of thought? Unamuno died in 1936, internationally famous, much quoted and exploited by foreign writers on Spain, but unknown to a wider public in spite of having been translated into a dozen languages. Within Spain, he had been isolated throughout his long life, attacked and courted, feared and misunderstood. Though he had many disciples and friends, he was the founder of no school, the centre of no movement. In politics he remained an erratic outsider. And yet the trace of his work and personality exists in the writings and in the minds of all younger Spaniards concerned with the problems of their country. It would be impossible to discuss modern Spain without turning to Unamuno as one of the main witnesses. Fourteen years after his death he is still alive as a great stimulator and questioner, more powerful than in his lifetime. This post-war world—or pre-war world—seems to have moved far away from Miguel de Unamuno, his Spanish problems and his work; certainly he seems forgotten. But our bitterest universal and individual conflicts are the real core of his writings, beneath all that is dated and localised in them.

Yet how to convey this, when Unamuno's books are so difficult to find except in the original, and when he was, as I suggested, an incarnation of the Spain of his time, which sounds like a contradiction of his claim to universality?

The task is made easier by the same qualities which constitute the weakness of his work. With passionate, self-centred energy Unamuno pursued a few basic problems through everything he wrote, through repetition, interpretation, exaggeration and contradiction. His search, not his results, was supremely important to him and to his exasperated, fascinated readers. Those problems were his own, but he conceived them also as the problems of other Spaniards, of his country as a whole, and of humanity; he made a doctrine out of this identification and a theory out of his self. In this, if in nothing else, he never changed. When he was fifty-two, he could rightly say: 'Without ever having laid claim to an absurd doctrinary consistency... I believe that there are few other publicists in Spain who have been so true to themselves in their essential and most intimate concerns. Strictly speaking, I have been developing a few fundamental thoughts, always the same, ever since I first began to write.' Thus, by following his monologue—or rather his interior duologue turned into written words—it will be possible to appraise Unamuno's subjective vision, and at the same time its Spanish and universally human significance.

First, however, it will be necessary to understand something of the society which shaped Unamuno's early emotions and ideas. This is necessary not only because Unamuno, like so many others, worked out his decisive early impressions in his later writings, but also because the problems he distilled from his adolescent experiences, eighty years ago, are still largely valid in present-day Spain.

Miguel de Unamuno was born in Bilbao in 1864, the son of a middle-class Basque family. That is to say, he was born and bred in a town where civic and spiritual conflicts were endemic. The official language, and the language of cultural life, was Castilian, but the ancient Basque was the mother tongue of a vast number of the inhabitants of Bilbao who spoke Spanish as a foreign language. What in most other Spanish provinces was merely regionalism-attachment to the *patria chica*, the 'little country', combined with indifference to the abstract idea of Spain and with distrust for the Madrid government, had in the Basque country grown into a nationalistic creed at once religious and political. The social structure of the Basque countryside was different from the rest of Spain, patriarchal rather than feudal. But Bilbao itself, though embedded in that rural society, was a rising industrial city and port, in touch with the outside world, with a liberal bourgeoisie and a vigorous working class; its leaders had a strong practical interest in the existence of a modern central administration.

At that time and in that place, Liberalism meant a somewhat superficial belief in constitutional government, mild reform, education, modern science and modern transport. It also meant an acute opposition to the powerful old-type clergy and to the tenets of the reactionary party which commanded the allegiance of the rural hinterland. This party, the Carlists or Traditionalists, hated modernism in any shape and stood for an absolute monarchy, a dominant Church in the spirit of the Inquisition, and for feudal virtues; they supported the younger branch of the Spanish Bourbon dynasty in its claim to the throne because Don Carlos, the pretender, would restore the true old Spain. Steeped in the tradition of the most hideous of Spain's interminable civil wars of the last century, the First Carlist War, 1833-1840, the Carlists believed in their right to use violence against the 'other Spain' of Liberals, Free-Masons and 'atheists'. Their chance came when the corrupt reign of Queen Isabella II was overthrown and a foreigner, Amadeus of Savoy, was called in as a constitutional King, only to be replaced by a short-lived, weak-rooted Republic which died of its own dissensions in 1874. The Second Carlist War lasted from 1870 till 1876, was fought against the armies of King Amadeus, of the Republic and of King Alfonso XII, and showed all the brutal violence of a community divided against itself. The situation was at its worst in the Basque country where the Carlists had their stronghold, while the towns, above all Bilbao, were Liberal.

Miguel de Unamuno, then a precocious boy, carried the scars of the conflict in his mind to his last day. His deepest impression was the siege of Bilbao when he was nine years old; the city was besieged and bombarded by the Carlists, defended by the Liberals (against a minority in their midst as well), and liberated by a Constitutionalist army. Twenty-four years later, Unamuno was to call his first novel, an epic of the Civil War, *Peace in War*.

But though the Carlists were defeated in the field and national unity restored by the newly established constitutional monarchy, the deeper schism within the nation continued. Banners and programmes changed; the Carlist party developed into a Traditionalist Basque movement, the regional Liberals merged with kindred groups throughout the country and built up a political machine in competition with the Conservatives; party jobbers flourished for two decades, while the more thoughtful leaders of both camps suggested remedies for the disease which was openly called 'Spain's decadence'. The social and psychological problems of the 'two Spains' eternally warring against each other became a matter for analytical essays: Conservative against progressive, orthodox against free-thinking, isolationist against europeanising—each diagnosis had its champions, each side its partisans. Yet the incurable split in the minds of countless Spaniards made nonsense of simplifying labels, whether they would admit it or not. Young Unamuno admitted it to himself: it became his obsession.

Unamuno was sixteen when he went to Madrid to take up his university studies in philosophy and ancient languages. As far as can be judged by his own reticent accounts, he seems to have tried to complement the meagre fare of his school education by avid reading, by absorbing any new message—and new messages came mainly from abroad—which might offer the key to intellectual integration. He reacted against his conventionally orthodox religious upbringing, but wanted to retain its essence even while responding to the stimulus of Protestant thinkers; he reacted against the narrow patriotism of the Basques, but longed for the gentle green of his native country and felt almost truculently a Basque himself; he wished to find a wider home in the Spain he dreamed of, but his first encounter with the capital disgusted him, and he rejected the Spain of the eighties. His student years were neither easy nor happy. University teaching in those times was barren, and Unamuno would not fit into any of the intellectual sets which formed around some dominant figures: neither into that of the most successful writer of the older generation, the polished, sceptical novelist Juan Valera; nor into that of the leading Conservative scholar and thinker, Don Marcelino Menendez y Pelayo, who believed in a renaissance of Spain through the revival of her missionary Catholic faith; nor into that of the enlightened Liberal educator Don Francisco Giner de los Ríos who fought for a renewal of Spain through free modern research, popular education and the training of an intellectual élite. Unamuno's later writings prove that he absorbed the ideas of both camps but considered their cures for his country's ills as mere palliatives, each of them half true and wholly insufficient. What he craved was a synthesis of the two Spains in his own conflict-ridden mind.

In a letter to the essayist Guillermo de Torre, Unamuno wrote, many years later, that in 1880 he had felt dissatisfied with the official textbook of metaphysics because it maintained that Hegel had denied the principle of contradiction, and that he therefore had started to learn German—by translating Hegel's

Logik. Nothing could have been more characteristic. Even at that early stage Unamuno not only questioned what was official and ready-made, as so many other adolescents have done, but also embarked all by himself on a voyage of intellectual discovery which, in the Spain of that time, was a hazardous adventure. And it was the logical problem of the contradictory which he wanted to solve—surely because he was driven by an unusual awareness of contradictions within himself.

But Unamuno's wrestling with Hegel was of more than psychological importance. Other foreign philosophers were to influence his thought profoundly, above all Kierkegaard, but for his own intellectual needs he adopted Hegel's dialectical method, transmuting it in a highly subjective manner. It permitted him to think, in terms not of final contradictions or antinomies, but of thesis and antithesis from which an inevitable synthesis was bound to come. The urge to express everything through this pattern lay even behind Unamuno's habitual, often tiresome paradoxes. If the synthesis eluded him, passionately though he believed in it, in this, too, he was a personification of his country.

After four years in Madrid, Unamuno returned to Bilbao, a graduate and scholar with unorthodox ideas, in search of a living and a public. He married, gave private classes and lectures, contributed anonymous articles to a local radical newspaper, took part in public discussions, wrote poetry, and learned foreign languages so as to be able to read authors in whom he had become interested through indifferent translations. Inspired by his childhood memories he collected material on the Second Carlist War, and applied in vain for several academic posts. Comparatively little is known about this period in Unamuno's life, least of all about his private life. His correspondence, as far as it has been published, indicates a sense of insecurity, and exasperation at the absence of any response in the stifling atmosphere of prosperous provincial philistinism. He felt a stranger in his own city. Even the beloved green countryside became a source of uneasiness. At least so it seemed to Unamuno four years later, after he had left Bilbao for Salamanca where he wrote his essay *En torno al casticismo* in 1895. There he gave a description of the austere Castilian tableland which was the setting of his new home, and contrasted its austere beauty and sadness, the perfect geometry of its horizon and the compact blueness of its skies, with the sensuous appeal of his native Basque countryside with its soft waves of lush meadows and leafy fields, inviting the soul to build a comfortable nest for itself and to indulge the appetites 'knit into the flesh since the dawn of time'.

There spoke a self-made puritan who felt, and fought, the soft pull of desires he deplored but could not wholly suppress. The gravest of Unamuno's inner conflicts during his vigorous manhood in Bilbao may have come not from his frustrated intellectual ambitions, but from his hankering for the more violent delights of life which his unrelenting conscience would not let him pursue. Certainly, once he had left his home country, he never seriously wished to live there, despite his professed and undoubted love for it; his turning away from the sensuous attractions of the Basque country was over-emphatic; when he visited Bilbao in later life, his attitude tended to be aggressive. All this cannot be simply explained, in the manner of some of his biographers, by the irritation of a prophet who felt misunderstood and underrated on his native soil. It seems to me to be part of Unamuno's protective armour against a temptation from which he had decided to flee in order to become what he wished to be, and which called loudest to him in the surroundings of his youth. There was more truth than exhibitionist pose in Unamuno's self-definition in a letter (to Leopoldo Alas) written in 1900: 'Unamuno is a self-torturer. He spends his life struggling to be what he is not, and failing.'

In 1891 Unamuno was successful in his application for the Chair of Greek at the University of Salamanca. It was the turning point of his career.

Life in the ancient city was calm, not to say stagnant; it was far more provincial and hide-bound than life in Bilbao, and not even the university itself, with all its impressive traditions, could have been called a centre of intellectual activities. To Unamuno, however, his new-won security, his academic success (he had to accept—unwillingly—another chair, that of Comparative Romance Philology, in addition to his first professorship), and even more the impact of the living tradition of Castile and the new perspective in which he now regarded the conflicts of his Basque years, brought a release of emotional and mental powers. He brimmed over with plans for works of poetry, imaginative prose and scholarship. He turned his philological lectures into exciting experiences for his students, by infusing them with his love and respect for the creative word. But the driving passion of those early years in Salamanca was his search for the image of a Spain that would rise triumphantly above petty divisions and nationalistic manœuvres, vindicating its human heritage and, incidentally, giving him a spiritual home. In the solemn landscape he found an inspiring symbol. As he put it: 'It is a monotheistic landscape, this infinite plain where a man is made small without losing his self, and where amid the parched fields he is made to feel the parched places in his soul'.

But Unamuno was no abstract dreamer. He saw everything clothed in flesh and blood. The essay in which he expressed his vision for the first time and which I have quoted before, *En torno al casticismo*, contained shrewd observation and analysis of the present as well, so that it became the most remarkable, though not the most noted, publication of the Spanish mid-nineties.

During a short stay in Madrid in 1891, while his appointment to Salamanca was pending, Unamuno had reviewed the political and cultural scene with a mature mind. He had made contact with others who, like himself, conceived the problem of Spain's existence as a nation and a modern State in terms of social ethics, not in terms of political technique after the fashion of leading statesmen. The most productive of those contacts was that with a brilliant young diplomat, Angel Ganivet. From Salamanca,

Unamuno kept up a correspondence with Ganivet; it helped both of them to a clarification of their ideas. The two essays which were in some part the fruit of this discussion, Ganivet's *Idearium español* (1896) and *En torno al casticismo* (1895), were to have an enormous influence on the next generation of Spanish intellectuals, once the shock of Spain's shattering defeat in the Cuban War of 1898 had done its work. At the time of the publication of Unamuno's essays in 1895, however, the response was a bitter disappointment to him. The fact that his message was hardly understood contributed to his increased vehemence and aggressiveness, above all in essays and articles. Soon he came to identify his struggle for an audience with the heart of the matter he wanted to convey; his tone grew more and more subjective. This makes *En torno al casticismo* all the more interesting, because there Unamuno was still comparatively detached and impersonal—as far as he ever could be impersonal in saying what to him was intrinsically, inevitably personal, his own and yet a universal truth. The essay is also important because it contains the nucleus of all Unamuno's ideas about Spain and the relation between nation and humanity, individual and nation; and finally it deserves particular attention because it transmits an impression of certain permanent aspects of Spanish society and of that elusive quality called the 'national character'. It is an impression which is slightly distorted and yet unusually clear, as though seen in a convex mirror.

The title itself, *En torno al casticismo*, defies translation, for the keyword, *casticismo*, was a topical slogan of the Spanish nineties, with specific mental and linguistic associations. *Lo castizo* means something typically and genuinely national within the Spanish orbit. When Unamuno attacked the cult of *lo castizo*, the *casticismo*, it was a fashion which covered a multitude of sins, a medley of tendencies. The central problem behind it was the position of Spain in Europe, in other words, the question whether to invite or reject foreign influences. The isolation of the country, cultural as well as political, had become painfully obvious. It could no longer be called a 'splendid isolation', since it had broken down in the economic field and Spanish governments had had to negotiate unfavourable international loans or grant humiliating industrial concessions to foreign groups. Even that weak beginning of industrialization changed the social pattern of the cities; the building of railways and roads changed the appearance as well as the outlook of the countryside. Two rising workers' movements, one anarchist, the other social-democratic, were in touch with brother organisations abroad and absorbed their ideas. Each newly established industry opened channels of communication, commercial and technical, with more highly industrialized countries. The times were past, though not forgotten, when Spanish universities shunned contact with foreign seats of learning, unless they were of unimpeachable religious orthodoxy, like Bologna or Leyden. The natural sciences had made a breach in the Chinese wall, and philosophy, letters and arts followed suit. A flood of translations (mostly of doubtful quality) brought a much-needed stimulus to the educated, though they remained out of reach for the mass of the people. The new contacts with the outside world emphasized the backwardness of Spain's social and cultural life when compared with the rest of Europe, and revealed her loss of prestige and power; yet they were not enough to bring about profound changes. They were enough, however, to rouse the antagonism of all those who wanted to preserve Spain's historic tradition, and above all her faith, from contagion by unsettling foreign ideas.

The battle between the *casticistas*, that is the apologists of a traditionally Spanish way of life, and the 'europeanisers' was joined. Inevitably, Conservatives, zealous Roman Catholics, and the leaders of backward rural communities were against any 'europeisation', while Liberals, anti-clericals, Socialists and modern business people—not a large number—were in its favour. At the same time the bulk of Spaniards, their perceptions blunted by their economic troubles or immunised by ignorance, were indifferent to the discussion which inflamed the minds of the vocal minority.

Their attitude was devastatingly assessed by Cánovas when he said that 'Spaniards are those who cannot be anything else'.

Unamuno brought a wholly new approach to the discussion. In the five articles which together constitute his *En torno al casticismo* he attacked the Traditionalists and *casticistas* not as a 'europeaniser', but as the defender of a new Spain, not yet born, against the outworn historical formulae, institutions and attitudes which threatened to stifle its birth. That new Spain, where all Spaniards would find their home, existed in the deeper layers of the Spanish mind; its 'eternal' tradition was transmitted and transformed by its people who never appeared on the surface of historic action. In the past it had been fed by influences from all the world and had in turn given values to the world. Hence there could be no contradiction between the 'genuinely Spanish' and the 'European': in their roots they were one and the same. If Traditionalists were afraid for their identity under the impact of foreign ideas, this only proved that their identity had already lost its substance. Spanish society would be revitalised by foreign ideas, foreign art, foreign challenge, not least from the Protestant countries; it had sunk into stagnation through the rigid seclusion imposed by the 'old ruling caste'. 'The eternal Spanish tradition which, being eternal, is human rather than Spanish, must be sought by us in the living present, not in the dead past,' said Unamuno. In the 'dead past' he included, daringly, the literature of Spain's so-called Golden Age in the sixteenth century. Its great works of art still had a message to give, but it had to be re-interpreted, otherwise it would bedevil the present. Above all Don Quixote and Sancho Panza, the lasting symbols of the dualism in the Castilian soul, had to be buried and resuscitated: not Don Quixote, the Knight Errant, but 'Alonso Quijano the Good', the simple human being Cervantes evoked at the end of his book, when madness falls away from Don Quixote in his hour of death, was the quintessence of the ideal Spaniard.

The 'historic caste' of Castile had created Spain, but Spain was not yet unified and not yet truly Spanish. To achieve integration meant an inward process which could only be obstructed by the false cult of *lo castizo*, with its confusion between form and substance. Religion was the strongest creative and unifying force, yet a formalist orthodoxy weakened the religious spirit. Not the Inquisition, set up in self-defence by the 'historic caste' as a kind of customs barrier, expressed the living faith of Spain at the height of her strength, but the Spanish mystics who were individualists, heterodox God-seekers despite their acceptance of ecclesiastic discipline, and—humanists.

From this analysis of the past, Unamuno turned to the Spanish present: 'A look at the present mental state of Spanish society shows us the old historic caste fighting against the new people . . . If we scratch the surface, we find an immanent, diffuse Inquisition at work . . .'

Spanish society was in a state of crisis. Internally there was growth, disruption and regrouping, but externally there was only a frightening 'marasmus', a wasting away of the body politic. Anarchy and hierarchy, egotism and formalism, pseudo-culture and hatred of ideas, vulgarity and paralysing gravity, young people but no youth, spiritual misery and political jobbery feeding on the anaemic social tissue 'like a polyp', and above everything a mortifying monotony and uniformity; thus Unamuno described the Spain of the mid-nineties. 'Meanwhile the domestic Inquisition, never fully defeated, is reappearing in defiance of civil liberties. Our national, authentically Spanish vices regain strength: lack of what the English call 'sympathy', the inability to understand and to take our neighbour such as he is . . .'

From this indictment Unamuno proceeded to the question: 'Is everything, then, moribund?' and answered it with a 'no'. The future of Spain was alive in her 'unknown people'. It would grow only when 'winds or whirlwinds from the European world wake it'. And his final answer to the problem of Spain versus Europe was: 'Spain has yet to be discovered, and only europeanised Spaniards will discover her.' This discovery would be made by the new youth of Spain.

Perhaps the strongest confirmation of Unamuno's judgement on the mental state of Spain was the reception with which his essay met. It fell virtually into a void. Indeed, if he was right in his assessment (and in summarising it, I had to omit many pertinent concrete observations) he could not have expected more than a lukewarm interest in small intellectual circles, enthusiasm of a handful of idealists, distrust among the Liberals who did not share his religious tenets, and hostility from the Traditionalists who scented a heretic in him. All this was his lot and he resented it. It is pathetic to read in Unamuno's letters to Leopoldo Alas how grateful he was for every scrap of praise for his essay. A still greater disappointment awaited him a couple of years later when he published his *Paz en la guerra*, the long novel on the Carlist War in which he meant to convey the living tradition of his own Basque 'caste'; it was an unmitigated (and not altogether undeserved) failure. Nevertheless, through *En torno al casticismo* Unamuno had established himself as a heterodox, controversial thinker and taken his stand in an isolation which was a source of strength as well as of vulnerability.

When a 'whirlwind' came from outside, in the shape of the Cuban War of 1898 in which Spain lost the last remnants of her overseas empire and which roused the whole younger generation to an acute awareness of the state of their country, Unamuno came into his own. That 'generation of "98" ', as it came to be called, went out to discover another Spain under the débris of the national earthquake, on roads Unamuno had shown. Its greatest lyric poet, Antonio Machado, owed his poetic vision of Castile, landscape and people, to the older man whose poetry had never matched the intensity of his thought; Azorin, soon the foremost 'Castilianist', elaborated in a much purer style and cooler tone what Unamuno had outlined in his first essay. Ten years later, Ortega y Gasset led a new movement of 'europeanisers' in the direction Unamuno had shown, and against Unamuno himself, who by then had changed his emphasis wholly to the 'inward tradition' because the modern mass movements seemed to him a new menace to his image of Spain. But whenever the 'old historic caste' or the 'domestic Inquisition' became particularly active and dangerous in their continual struggle against the nascent new Spain, Unamuno raised a voice which could no longer be ignored. The fundamental position he had taken in *En torno al casticismo* remained the key to his public action as a Spaniard.

II

The Tragic Sense of Life

In his introduction to an anthology of Unamuno's prose, published in England[1], Professor J. B. Trend exclaimed: "but how can an introducer do justice to the zig-zags of Unamuno's thought: to a prose-writer whom such a master of verse as Rubén Darío could describe as being before all things a poet, to a prophet who 'believed that he believed, but did not really believe', to a philosopher who took up the most contradictory positions one after the other?" To this, Unamuno would have given his favourite answer that the contradictions existed in the mind of the reader, not in his own. But the 'zig-zags of his thought' in the decade after *En torno al casticismo* are at first glance bewildering. They are also illuminating: they correspond to important changes in him and to a chronic state of conflict in Spain.

The year 1898, the year of the Cuban defeat, affected Unamuno in a different way from most other Spaniards. As he could not believe that the existence of a nation depended on its external power and prestige, he lost no illusions through a military and diplomatic débâcle which did not come as a surprise. All those Spaniards who had been educated in the traditional atmosphere of 'Imperial Spain' and took it for granted that they belonged to a glorious nation, to their own greater glory, now discovered to their humiliation that their country was no match for the new great powers. The shock produced the natural reaction. Yet Unamuno realised that this kind of offended vainglory affected only the upper and middle class, while the people were the same as before, secure in what he called their 'eternal tradition'. His image of Spain demanded no revision after defeat. He found that two forms of public hypocrisy were rampant. One expressed itself in

[1] Miguel de Unamuno: *Prosa diversa,* Selection by J. L. Gili, London 1938, The Dolphin Bookshop Editions; New York, 1939.

patriotic lucubrations about lost honour, and so forth; the other in clamouring for 'regeneration' through quick, superficial changes after the model of other European countries, regardless of Spain's social structure. He lashed out against both sides, but, in contrast to his previous position, the heavier blows fell on the modernisers.

An article written in 1898 before the end of the war, *La crisis del patriotismo*, still continued the main line of *En torno al casticismo*. Propaganda for 'that sorry sort of national honour' which was bound up with war had become a weapon of the new bourgeoisie; nationalism, as far as it was not a literary invention of 'the great urban centres', was imposed by the great landowners; both served to exploit the 'silent people'. The crisis of patriotism was in reality a process of polarization: on the one side a growing cosmopolitan sentiment in the industrialized sector, on the other side an intensified adherence to the 'small native region' among the country people who 'sought refuge in their home parishes from the brutality of capitalism'. A genuine patriotism—love for the country, not aggressive nationalism—would come from a synthesis of both.

In another article written in the same year, after the defeat, Unamuno discussed the topic of Spain's regeneration under the title of *La vida es sueño (Life is a Dream)*. Gone was the wish for a synthesis between the progressive cosmopolitanism of the towns and the healthy local traditions of the countryside. It was a passionate defence of the right of simple people to go on living their lives as in a dream without being forced into what the modern mind calls wakefulness:

> Strictly speaking, only we so-called intellectuals and a handful of public men speak on every occasion about the regeneration of Spain . . . The people, the mass of private individuals or *idiots*, as the Greeks used to call them, the *hoi polloi* of Plato, fail to respond. They hear all that talk as one may listen to the rain dripping . . . At the outbreak of the war many sons were taken from their fathers who let them go with comparative

calm because it meant a way out; they would have had to emigrate otherwise. What difference between dying in a war or dying elsewhere? . . . Death frightens only the intellectuals, sick as they are with longing for immortality, and terrified by the nothing beyond life on earth which their logic presents to them . . . Now they come to the people with the catchphrase of regeneration, determined to wake them up from their dreams. They say the people suffer from *aboulia*, from lack of will, that there is no national consciousness . . . Let the people sleep and dream their slow, dark, monotonous dream of a good life! Don't sacrifice them to progress—for God's sake, don't sacrifice them to progress!

This shows the turn Unamuno's thought was taking when the general crisis drove him more and more into himself. He envied the Spanish peasants their Christian acceptance of the rhythm of life and death because he had become agonizingly conscious of his own fear of death and nothingness, perhaps through the atmosphere of death which the war spread everywhere. The peasants' faith in 'eternal reality' could not be his, because his logic confronted him with its contradiction; but from the abyss of his doubts he wanted to preserve others from such doubts, almost as a consolation for himself. If progress were to mean liberation from the oppressiveness of material needs, and freedom to discover the eternal needs of the spirit, then he would have welcomed even its mechanic tools; but he rejected progress as an ideal for its own sake, or as a means to further some abstract interest of the nation at the expense of people of flesh and blood. Spain's national catastrophe had not made Unamuno less radically antagonistic to those who 'took the name of the Faith in vain to speak to the people of a historic Spain conquering realms where neither the sun nor injustice ever set'. It had, however, turned him against the kind of empty 'progressive' patter which obscured what to him had become the vital issue: his personal faith, the faith in survival for which he had to fight against himself. This would have left him once again in deadly isolation, had he not converted his problem into that of all Spaniards.

In the years that followed he was to re-state it again and again in varying terms, always with the conviction that he spoke for every human being in speaking of himself, and that he had to speak as a man rooted in his soil, as the Spaniard of Basque origin, if he wished to express a concrete human truth. The evolution of his thought was marked by three books or great essays, more professions of faith than philosophical treatises: *Vida de Don Quijote y Sancho* (1905), *Del sentimiento trágico de la vida en los hombres y en los pueblos* (1913), and *La agonía del cristianismo* (1931). But as a counterpoint, an endless stream of articles, poems and tales reflected his changing emotions and changing reactions to himself and others.

It may seem odd to attach such importance to a journalistic output which was so immense in quantity that one would have expected it to be ephemeral: Unamuno himself calculated that he had written something like four thousand articles between 1880 and 1924, and after 1924 his rate of production did not slacken. It may also seem odd that the head of a famous old university (Unamuno was Rector of Salamanca from 1901 till 1914, and again from 1931 till his death in 1936) should never have ceased work as an active journalist, though in this case it meant not only short essays, sketches and book reviews, but above all polemic, implicitly or explicitly political polemic. These apparent oddities demand an explanation.

The simplest reason, a very powerful one, was financial. The salaries of academic teachers in Spain were so low that the authorities took it for granted that they were being supplemented by alternative sources of income. Poets and writers were in a similar position. As long as the Spanish reading public was, through wide-spread illiteracy, half-illiteracy and a low standard of living, so pitifully small, very few writers managed to live on their royalties from books. Unamuno was not the only professor and serious writer who turned to journalism at an early stage. Journalism was, for the same social and economic reasons, not exactly lucrative either, but it provided publicity and a tribune. Intellectual snobbery about 'mere journalism' did not yet exist; and neither material conditions nor the atmosphere of political tension which permeated everything permitted a withdrawal into an ivory tower.

Unamuno despised empty or demagogical journalism, but he quickly grasped the value of public controversy through the press and the advantage of being 'topical' if he wanted to get a hearing for his ideas. He laid himself deliberately open to attacks by exaggerating his own case against any form of mental laziness or conformism, of sterile fanaticism or smug hypocrisy. This, of course, meant that Unamuno made sallies in all directions, often repeating himself, contradicting himself, but always returning to his central position, and always stimulating others to carry on where he had ended an argument.

Let me take one example from many: Unamuno's attitude to rural backwardness and urban civilization in some of its shifting aspects. It is a good example because it shows how he linked a social or political problem to his all-important quest for a faith. In *La vida es sueño* Unamuno had praised the dumb wisdom of peasants and cried out against the progress which would make them 'articulate'. That was in 1898, when the modernizers seemed in the ascendant. In 1904, when politicians, particularly Conservatives, extolled the uneducated masses to whom they owed their electoral victories, Unamuno declared in an article on 'Public Opinion' that the alleged democracy was a rule of illiterates, at that time forty-nine percent of the adult population, who voted like sheep. He went so far as to demand that they should be deprived of their votes because they 'had neither opinions nor any social understanding of their own, outside the immediate needs of their existence, outside their struggle for their daily bread'. In 1907, after another Government victory at the polls, he made still clearer what he thought of rural ignorance as a civic virtue. In *Civilización es civismo (Civilization is Civism)* he wrote:

The immense majority of staunch deputies on the Government side—this time Conservatives or, better, reactionaries—come from the rural districts. The opposition comes from the cities which form the only conscious element in Spain at present. The countryside is generally submerged in ignorance, backwardness and avarice . . . The villager is greedy and mean. And he is sadly unconscious. Large numbers of villagers do not know who governs them. They believe neither in the Law nor in its efficacy.

He argued that in Liberal Salamanca, hungry workmen refused the bribes offered for their votes, while farmers in the surrounding villages sold themselves for a pittance. Even in his own Basque country the small townships were morally better than the hamlets, where cases of 'sordid ruthlessness' abounded.

But in 1909 he took part in a homage to Darwin (whom he greatly respected) and was frightened by the 'anti-Christian' interpretation workers had given to the science of evolution. In the article *Materialismo popular* he explained that he was in favour of economic and social reform as long as it did not destroy the preoccupation with God and immortality. He was not worried by the fact that people lost their orthodox beliefs, but by the weakening of their desire for a personal after-life, while he 'carried that thorn in the depth of his heart'. To be told that man lived on through his deeds, his children, and his contribution towards a better human society, appeared to him as 'the most miserable subterfuge to escape from profound despair', the despair at not being able to believe in immortality. He noted that people brought up in the Roman Catholic faith, like the Spanish workers, were prone to accept the shallowest tenets of materialism. Minds formed by the legacy of centuries of 'ritualistic, authoritarian religion' were in danger of falling 'from the ridiculous, infantile Heaven and Hell of superstition into the gross superstition of the mere Here and Now'. If that was the fruit of reading, then he, the champion of culture for the Spanish people, began to doubt whether it was right to teach the workers to read.

This particular zig-zag line of thought led Unamuno from a first implicit expression of his own fear of death to an explicit personal confession. In 1898 his concern appears to have been to spare others the tortures of his own doubt; by 1909 he had come to wish that all others should share his despair. Simultaneously he had become more definite in his social ideas, more ready to intervene in any political matter which roused his civic conscience, and an adversary of the Conservative-monarchic system, however grave remained his criticism of the Left. He had shaped his written and spoken word so that it fitted his idea of himself: 'The best part of my work has always been to disturb my neighbours, to harrow them out of the lethargy of their hearts', he said in the essay *My Religion*, in 1907.

In this spirit Unamuno wrote his most disturbing work: *The Tragic Sense of Life in Men and Peoples.* A book that was not meant as an orderly philosophical treatise on the human condition, but as one man's record of his thoughts on life and death, confessed before his fellow-mortals with all the passionate sincerity of which that man was capable, does not lend itself easily to summarization. It stands or falls with the sympathy it evokes: sympathy in the sense of sharing the emotion behind the argument. *The Tragic Sense of Life* is the greatest of the many monologues Unamuno wrote. Every bit of reasoning in it springs from his intimate spiritual needs; nothing is 'objective'. This is as he meant it to be, and he argues at the very beginning of the book that this subjectivity is the only truthful approach possible. In consequence, the long disquisitions on philosophical systems and religious doctrines are far less important than the self-revelation, which has a strangely moving poetic force, despite its harsh, massive style. One may reject Unamuno's reasoning and approach; one may become irritated when he dismisses impatiently any thought which could dissolve or solve his tragic conflict; one may find his stubborn obsession morbid or merely of psychological interest as a sample of Spanish ideology; but hardly anyone will be able to remain untouched when Unamuno speaks of his longings and fears. For the urge to find a meaning in life and the fear of absolute futility are surely alive in the mind of every human being.

This is the problem as Unamuno poses it:

> Why do I want to know whence I have come and where I shall go, whence those around me have come and where they will go, and what it all means? It is because I do not want to die altogether, and I want to know whether I must or must not die for ever. And if I die not, what will become of me? If I die, nothing has any meaning any more. There are three possible solutions: (a) that I know for certain that I have to die altogether, and then the despair is incurable; (b) that I know I shall not die altogether, and then it is resignation; (c) that I cannot know either way, and then it means resignation within the despair, or despair within resignation, a desperate resignation or a resigned despair, and–struggle.

Even in the posing of the problem, there are certain highly personal aspects. To Unamuno it was inconceivable that anybody should not feel black despair at the thought of death as the end; it was equally inconceivable to him to feel something better than resignation at the thought that he would not die altogether, but 'only' lose his body; and, as he said elsewhere, an impersonal survival, a return to the Great Absolute, would make all things meaningless for him. This defence of his personality had been part of his inner life since his childhood:

> Of myself, I can say that as a boy and even as a child I was unmoved by the awesome descriptions of Hell I was given, because already then nothing seemed more horrible to me than the Nothing. It was a furious hunger to be . . .

Unamuno's 'hunger to be' would not be stilled by the teachings of his faith because he wanted not only to believe but to 'know'. Hence the need to test all answers to the problem with his intellect, but always in the light of his un-rational urges.

At the beginning of his book, Unamuno challenges all abstract and objective philosophers: the only legitimate subject and supreme object of philosophy is the man of flesh and blood (the Spanish idiom is 'flesh and bone') the living, breathing, unique individual, but not Man in the abstract. Philosophy fulfils a human need to see life and the world as a whole; it grows from our sentiment towards life. That sentiment has unconscious or sub-conscious roots. Once this is realised, the individual man with his intimate problems can be discerned in every philosophical system, however impersonal his conscious reason may have made it appear. The man Kant built up with his heart, in the *Critique of Practical Reason*, what his brain had torn down. The man Spinoza erected a whole edifice of thought to console himself for his lack of faith in his personal immortality: 'You and I and Spinoza, we wish never to die, and that desire is our very essence'. To pursue truth for its own sake is inhuman; pure knowledge is no end in itself; the starting point for every philosophy which is more than philosophizing must be 'real and practical'; that is to say it must have a purpose. The purpose is to help men and their society, to help men in their attitude to life and in their consciousness. The most tragic problem of philosophy is that it must try to conciliate the intellectual needs of men with their emotional and volitive needs. Any philosophy that pretends to dissolve the tragic contradiction at the root of our existence must fail. Hunger for personal immortality and the endeavour to continue indefinitely as a definite being is the motive behind all our search for cause and finality. 'And thus all philosophy and all religion have their personal, affective starting point in the tragic sense of life.'

No man can imagine himself as non-existent. He not only desires immortality but wants to go on growing within immortality.

The visible universe . . . becomes narrow for me, like a cage so small that my soul hits against its bars in her flights; I have not enough air to breathe. More, more and still more! I want to be my self, and without ceasing to be my self, to be all others as well, to penetrate into all things visible and invisible, to extend myself into the limitless space and to prolong myself into the time without end. If I am not all and for ever, it is as though I were nothing. And at least to be my whole self and to be it for ever after! And being whole myself, all the others are. Either all or nothing.

Pg. 26

When we are attacked by doubt of the immortality of our souls, we grow anxious to attain a shadow of immortality. We want to be outstanding so that something of ourselves may survive in the memory of others, and this desire turns to vanity, greed and terrible envy. 'Envy is a thousand times more terrible than hunger, because it is spiritual hunger. If what we call the problem of existence, that of the daily bread, is solved, our earth will be hell, for then the struggle for survival will become more violent.'

Many, above all simple people, slake their thirst for eternity in the fountain of religious faith, but 'to drink there is not given to all'. The institution which has for its primary purpose to protect that faith in the immortal soul is the Catholic Church. But 'Catholicism wanted to rationalize that faith by turning religion into theology, by basing the vital creed on a philosophy, and a philosophy of the thirteenth century at that'.

The chapter of *The Tragic Sense of Life* which discusses the Roman Catholic solution of the 'vital problem', the hunger for immortality, is curiously ambiguous. In a long analysis of the historic growth of doctrine and organisation, Unamuno shifts continuously from praise to attack, from acceptance to irony. As the belief in a life after death is vital, he wants to believe (but does not say he believes) in the dogma of Resurrection and the sacrament of the Eucharist, the 'bread of immortality' which is the core of popular Catholic piety. Whatever the 'ethical deviation' of theology might say, Redemption is 'to save us from death rather than from sin'. Thanks to confession, Catholics have been less preoccupied with sin than the Protestants. True, 'religion had to be converted into a police for the benefit of society', and the concept of Hell followed from it. But at the last analysis, 'the important thing is not to die, whether sinning or not'.

Because a simple, unreasoning faith stands for life, the countless difficulties of a rational order weigh nothing against the life-giving sentiment. In this sense the Church has been right in trying to stem the tide of rationalism, even when it meant victimizing Galileo because his discovery threatened to shake the belief that man was the centre of the universe.

There is self-punishment as well as dry sarcasm in the words:

> The true sin, perhaps the unforgivable sin against the Holy Ghost, is the sin of heresy, of thinking for oneself. Here in our Spain it has been said that to be a Liberal, hence a heretic, is worse than being a murderer, thief or adulterer. The gravest sin is that of not obeying the Church whose infallibility protects us from reason. And why should one be outraged by the infallibility of a man, the Pope? What difference is there between the infallibility of a book, the Bible, that of a society of men, the Church, and that of a single man?

But alas, the enemy is within the castle. Faith, not being secure in itself, nor secure in tradition and authority, seeks the support of 'its enemy, reason'. This was the origin of the theology of the Schools, and later 'natural theology, which is but an emasculated Christianism'. Thomist philosophy was brought in to prove that the dogma, if super-rational, was at least not anti-rational; by now not only the dogmas but also their 'medieval and Thomist interpretation' have to be accepted. Catholic dogmatism it a system of more or less reconciled contradictions which give it a profound 'vital dialectic'. But it costs dear: nothing less than the suppression of the mental needs of believers with an adult reason is the price. They are asked to believe everything or nothing, with the result that, particularly in France and Spain, enormous numbers of people are driven from anti-Papism to utter atheism. There is a terrible danger of revulsion in having to believe too much. Yet an even worse danger is that of wanting to believe with one's reason instead of 'with life'.

Unamuno reaches the conclusion that the Catholic solution of the vital problem—the problem of immortality and the eternal salvation of the individual soul—satisfies the will and the sense of life. But because of its rationalization by dogmatic theology, it fails to satisfy reason. And 'reason has its exigencies, as imperious as those of life itself'. Unamuno was an anti-rationalist and vitalist (and an existentialist, personalist and pragmatist, if one wishes to apply labels) but he believed in the proper use of reason, and could not bring himself to accept rational arguments which to him seemed anti-rational. Nor did he think that anybody who lacked the simple, robust faith of 'a charcoal-burner' could be turned into a charcoal-burner at will. Thus he confessed himself to be one of those to whom it was not given to drink from the fountain of faith, at least not as it was dispensed by the Roman Catholic Church in which he had grown up and to which he belonged, irrevocably, heterodox or heretic though he was.

Yet Unamuno's struggle for his belief in God and Christianity begins in this book, as it did in his life, at the point where he leaves theological dogmatism behind. Not in *The Tragic Sense of Life*, but in the earlier essay *My Religion* he puts it in a comparatively simple, direct form:

> My religion is to seek truth in life and life in truth, though in the knowledge that I shall not find them while I live; my religion is to struggle incessantly and tirelessly with the mystery; my religion is to wrestle with God from daybreak to nightfall, as they say Jacob wrestled with him . . . Emotionally, with my heart and feeling, I have a strong tendency toward Christianity, without subscribing to the specific dogmas of this or that

Christian denomination . . . And if I believe in God, or at least believe that I believe in Him, it is above all because I want Him to exist, and then because He reveals himself to me, through my heart, in the Gospel and in Christ and in history. This is a matter of the heart. Which means that I am not convinced of it as I am of two and two making four.

Hume is right, says Unamuno, when he concludes that the immortality of the soul cannot be proved rationally. It is also true that, within limits, it can be proved rationally that individual consciousness ends with the organism on which it depends. For our reason only that is true which is demonstrable; whether that truth means consolation or despair does not matter—'intelligence is a terrible thing'. But, he asks, is there not another truth than rational truth? The worst of the scientific rationalists are those who try to make others forget their hunger for immortality and fob them off with substitutes, as though, in their disbelief, they resented that others should believe, or even that others should wish to believe in another life after death. 'The physical eunuch does not feel the need to reproduce himself in the flesh, the spiritual eunuch does not feel the hunger to perpetuate himself.' The great rationalist philosophers, however, like Spinoza, were 'madly hungry for eternity'. Their exploration of the limits of reason leads in the end to a dissolution of reason itself, to doubt in its validity, to absolute relativism and scepticism. In that abyss, rational scepticism and emotional despair, 'the noblest, deepest, most fecund and most human state of the mind there is', meet and clash. And in their clash is the beginning of a new hope, though a terrible beginning.

The chapter, or rather essay, in *The Tragic Sense of Life* which Unamuno calls *At the Bottom of the Abyss* is the heart of the book. He sums up again: faith in immortality is irrational, and yet 'life, faith and reason' all need each other. After the Middle Ages with their ardent faith that was in its deepest core desperate, and not without profound uncertainties, our society entered into the age of rationalism with its new uncertainties. In the words of Browning, in *Bishop Blougram's Apology:*

> All we have gained then by our disbelief
> Is a life of doubt diversified by despair
> For one of faith diversified by doubt.

Doubt, uncertainty, vacillation between two questions—'Is it?' and 'Is it not?'—are the basis of our intimate life. Affirmation, denial, and the refusal to affirm or deny, all spring from despair. Even in Pascal's Jansenism and in the doctrines of Ignatius de Loyola is a sediment of religious desperation which led Pascal to a 'suicide of reason' and Ignatius to the killing of reason by discipline. Once the great obstacle, reason, is overcome, and faith regained in the existence of personal consciousness after death, even if burdened by uncertainty and anguish, imagination is set free.

At this point Unamuno interrupts himself and addresses the reader:

> I did not want to keep silence where others keep silent; I wanted to lay bare, not merely my own soul, but the human soul, be it what it may, be it destined to disappear or not. And so we have reached the bottom of the abyss, the irreconcilable conflict between reason and the vital sense. And at this point I have told you that we must accept the conflict as such and live by it. Now it remains for me to explain how, according to my feelings and even to my thought, that despair can become the basis of a vigorous life, of effective action, of ethics, aesthetics, religion, and logic too . . . Finally I shall maintain that the religious desperation of which I spoke to you, and which is nothing but the tragic sense of life itself, is more or less disguisedly the background of the consciousness of the individuals and the cultured peoples in these our days—that is to say, of those individuals and those peoples which suffer neither from

> intellectual nor from sentimental stupidity . . . And if thereby I can confirm and sustain the same desire in someone else, perhaps when it was dwindling in him, then I shall have done a human work and, above all, I shall have lived. In short, with, without or against reason, I do not want to die. And when I finally die, if it were to mean a total death, I shall not have let myself die, but I shall be killed by the destiny of man. I do not resign from life . . . And as to truth, the true truth independent of ourselves, outside our heart and our logic—who knows what it may be?

This is the summing up of this book, of the man Unamuno, his life's work and his life. Everything else in *The Tragic Sense of Life* flows from it.

Unamuno goes on to build up his vision of practical life, his own religion and his psychology on the basis of the all-pervading contradiction. He describes how spiritual love springs from physical love through compassion and shared suffering, and how compassion shapes the personality, how it creates respect for personality and personalises everything. The God he wants to exist must be a personal God, not an impersonal, unconscious force. The after-life loses its meaning for him if the essence of personality is lost: he would prefer Purgatory with its unending hope to a final state of quiet in the Glory. Paraphrasing a passage in Sénancour's *Obermann*, he reaches his form of the categorical imperative: 'Let us act so that the Nothing becomes an injustice. Let us battle against destiny even if there is no hope of victory. Let us battle against it quixotically.'

He questions what he has written, forestalling the critics who would accuse him of a destructive approach, and confesses:

> But it is my task—I was going to say my mission—to shatter the faith of the one, of the other, and of the third, the faith in affirmation, the faith in negation and the faith in abstention, and to do this out of faith in faith itself. It is my task to fight

> against all those who resign themselves, be it against Catholicism or Rationalism or Agnosticism. It is my task to make all live in unquiet and longing.

At the end, Unamuno says, and has the right to say, that the tragic sense he attributed to 'men and peoples' is at least alive in Spaniards as individuals and in the Spanish people, reflected as it is in his own consciousness 'which is a Spanish consciousness, made in Spain.'

III

The Poet in Unamuno

Unamuno had an ardent wish to be recognised as a great poet in verse and prose. He insisted on an assessment of his writings which his greatest admirers were unable to endorse; for instance, he gave pride of place to his first novel, *Peace in War*, and he maintained that he would be best remembered by his poetry. His rough-tongued poems with their blend of fervour and contemplation brought indeed a new note into Spanish lyrical poetry at the turn of the century, but their poetic form was never strong enough to absorb the sentiments and thoughts that inspired them. It was not Unamuno himself who found the right lyrical shape for his visions, but his much younger friend Antonio Machado. And yet Unamuno was not wrong when he called himself a poet: he was a poet who had to create a world in his image so as to assure himself of his self. Taken in this sense, Unamuno's true poetic creation was the personality he projected into all his work; his 'agony', his ceaseless struggle with himself and the universe, was the core of every one of his novels and stories, poems and essays.

If he sometimes failed as an artist, it was because he handled his tools clumsily; he often insisted on the rights of his thesis against the intrinsic demands of the tale which was to clothe it. What he wanted to write was not something that made 'good reading', but something that penetrated below the surface to truth. And though he always spoke of 'men of flesh and blood' the people he created in his novels often remained shadows of himself, because the truth he pursued was his own personal truth. He made a virtue out of his necessity and defended his imaginative prose by attacking its critics as formalists and superficial materialists; his creatures were himself, he would say, and this was only right and true; he neglected the material side in his narration because he was intent on conjuring up the 'spirit of flesh, bone, rock, water and cloud' and therefore the 'true and intimate reality'. This, then, is the yardstick by which he wanted his novels to be measured, and it is the same as that which he accepted for his subjective philosophy. Unamuno's vision was indivisible; just as the man cannot be separated from his edifice of thought, his fiction or poetry cannot be separated from his philosophy.

To a certain degree, his first attempt at writing a novel, *Peace in War*, is an exception. At that period of his life he had not yet made the internal conflict his source of strength. The hero with whom Unamuno is identified still rejects the principle of 'all or nothing' as the temptation of Lucifer; he still hopes for peace within himself. It has to be admitted that the descriptive passages in the novel are heavy, its objective realism almost dull.

Unamuno's next novel was published five years later, in 1902, when he had already discovered that he had to renounce peace for war. This second novel was called *Amor y pedagogía (Love and Pedagogy)* and was, intrinsically, a personal pamphlet against the claims of science. The hero sets himself the task of engendering, rearing and educating a son 'scientifically', so that he will be a perfect man and great scientist. Though he loves his son, he imposes a programme on him which is inhuman and absurd. His failure is obvious: the son ends by suicide. The work is weak and freakish. The protagonist is an exaggerated example of the ignorant crank who derives his notions of science from the worst kind of popular pseudo-scientific literature. This might have been a comic portrait or a trenchant satire, but it is overdone, and the tragic ending belies the structure of the narration. It fits, however, Unamuno's tragic view of the underlying problem. On one level, he deplored and feared the fashionable popular abuse of scientific slogans; on a deeper level, he feared and hated science as soon as it threatened his anti-rational sense of life. And yet Unamuno had an enormous respect for science within the limits he was willing to grant it. So his novel shows not science, but the distortion of science, as a killing force. The unsolved artistic discrepancy in the book points at an unsolved discrepancy in the mind of its author.

Between *Amor y pedagogía* and Unamuno's third and most publicized novel, *Niebla (Mist)*, lie twelve years of struggle and achievement. *Niebla* came out in 1914, the year in which Unamuno was relieved of his post as Rector of Salamanca University because of his continual polemics against the régime, and in which the discussion started by his *Tragic Sense of Life*, published the year before, was gathering strength. By then Unamuno was internationally famous; in Spain he was, with all that this implies in authority and loneliness, the grand old man of letters at the comparatively early age of fifty. He had succeeded in his rôle as disturber and challenger of settled beliefs, he had raised his spiritual problems to the level of an all-embracing personalist view of the world (his fury at the mere suggestion of hard-and-fast 'theories' forbids the term one would naturally use in the case of another thinker), but as a poet and novelist he had fallen short of his ambitions.

In *Niebla* he attempted not only to pose his eternal tragic question in an imaginative form, but also to establish the full significance of his disregard for more conventional standards of novel-writing. If his novels were neither realistic nor psychological in the then prevailing fashion, nor exercises in fantastic fiction, this was because he created another reality by 'realizing himself' in imagined beings who had a life of their own, yet were part of himself. The world of his personages was more real for him than the world of public figures he had known, because through them he made himself live. But beneath both those worlds, the one called real and the other into which he had projected himself, was the 'world of consciousness without space or time'. He, Unamuno, was as much or as little 'fiction' as the personages of his novels, because he, too, would die—or live. He dreamed dreams of himself and others, was 'dreamt by others', and the living dream was the immortality he demanded for himself *and* those others. He demanded it, too, for the figures of his imagination: the reader had to re-create them within himself. Therefore his novels needed no scenery or description, only characters who lived their lives according to their spiritual laws. The right place for descriptions of landscape and customs was, Unamuno insisted again and again, in his travel books and essays. His novels, however, went together with 'philosophy and theology', as he put it in one of his many forewords (which were as provocative as those of Bernard Shaw, though usually shorter).

Unamuno shared with Bernard Shaw not only a liking for self-explanation and for rambling yet pungent discussion by means of forewords, but also a shrewd sense of publicity. He drove home the point he wanted to make in *Niebla*—that is to say, its literary point—through a sub-title which became a slogan. He called the book not a novel (in Spanish *novela*) but a 'nivola'. *Nivola* is a word invented in the spirit of Lewis Carroll, and also, paradoxically, in the spirit of James Joyce: it uses two assonances, one with *niebla*—fog or mist—and one with *novela*, to provoke mental associations with both. It was as if Unamuno wanted to say that his novels created a reality out of the mist of everyday existence; he admitted that it was partly a joke and partly a calculated stunt, highly successful at that, but a stunt with a serious meaning to it as well. In the foreword to the second edition of *Niebla* (1935) he expressed it as follows:

> Augusto Pérez (i.e. the hero of *Niebla*) warns all of us, all those who were and are I, all of us who represent the dream of God . . . that we shall have to die. They are dying for me in the flesh that exists in space, but not in the flesh of the dream, the flesh of consciousness. And therefore I tell you, readers of my *Niebla*, dreamers of my Augusto Pérez and his world, that this is the mist, this is the *nivola*, this is legend, history, and eternal life.

Compared to the weight of thought and philosophical intention Unamuno put into this *nivola*, the plot of the story is not very important. The hero is another tortured being, hungry for an affection which is denied to him. Augusto Pérez dreams of a perfect home and perfect love after the death of his mother who had kept him wrapped up in tenderness and romantic idealism. The woman with whom he falls in love is herself in love with a callous egotist; she is practically-minded, hates her precarious economic situation and her profession of piano teacher, and accepts Augusto's quixotic offers of help also for the sake of her ne'er-do-well lover Mauricio. The pressure of public opinion in the small town makes it impossible to do what Augusto had planned for her happiness. He had been willing to make it financially possible for her to marry Mauricio, while keeping her friendship for himself, but she subtly pushes him into an offer of marriage which, in the circumstances, seems to her in her own best interest. Augusto dreams of a fulfilment of his hopes. But Eugenia, once her material problem is solved, cannot go through with the marriage; to her, Augusto is nothing but a weak fool, all her imagination as well as all her feeling is bound up with Mauricio. On the eve of the wedding the two elope, leaving a cynical letter behind, and Augusto decides to commit suicide.

At this point of the story, Unamuno breaks off the thread and confronts his Augusto with himself, the author, in a way which anticipates Pirandello's *Six Characters in Search of an Author*. (The kinship between Unamuno and Pirandello, most obvious in their tragi-comic twists and their subjectivism, has often been noted; it was seven years after the publication of *Niebla*, in 1921, when Pirandello's play created a fashion, that Unamuno's *nivola* began to enjoy a certain vogue through translations, the first of them into Italian.) The conversation between Unamuno and Augusto is a paraphrase of passages from *The Tragic Sense of Life*. The author tells his personage that he is unable to kill himself because he is not alive except as a fictitious being, bound by the intentions of his maker. This Augusto denies: 'Isn't it rather you than I, my dear Don Miguel, who is a fictitious being, neither alive nor dead?' The author, he claims, cannot make his personages do what he likes; he does not even know them well. All the same, Unamuno decrees that Augusto has to die, but not by his own action. Augusto rebels; now that he is condemned to death, he wants to live, only to live, even if another Eugenia and another Mauricio make a mockery of him:

> So you do not want me to be myself, to get out of the fog, to live, live, see myself, hear myself, feel my pain, to be me? So I have to die as a fictitious being? All right, my lord creator, Don Miguel, you too will die and return to the nothing whence you came. God will cease to dream you! You will die, yes, even if you don't want to; you will die and all who read my story will die, all, all, not one will remain. Beings of fiction like me . . . To create so as to let me die! You will die too. Who creates, creates himself, and who creates himself, dies himself.

Augusto goes home in despair and wants to forget his trouble in sleep. 'But', he asks his servant, 'have I never done anything but sleep and dream? Has all this been nothing more than fog?'

When the author hears that his character has died, he repents and thinks of resurrecting him. But Augusto appears to him in a dream, and tells him that a resurrection is impossible. A fictitious as well as a 'real' being can be engendered and can be killed. But once dead, not even the maker-dreamer can resuscitate him, for 'one does not dream the same dream twice; what you dream and believe to be me would yet be another'.

Here Unamuno does not shirk an accusation of blasphemy. The literary experiment is a philosophical experiment. There is an exact parallelism, to his mind, between, on the one hand, an author and his literary personage, and, on the other, between the author and God. Can God create beings, kill them, and then resurrect them, he asks, and gives himself the answer which sums up his 'abysmal despair': no, because the resurrected being would not be the same, even though God himself, the Creator, may believe it. And there he leaves the reader, leaves him in a fog, without even a glimmer of that mystical hope which was to emerge from some of his later *nivolas*.

It should be clear from the outline I have given that *Niebla* is by no means a perfect literary vehicle to carry all this burden. It achieves its one purpose, to stir the reader's mind, but for most of us it fails to stir the imagination and make us 'realise' the characters. But in this failure there is a triumph for Unamuno: it is once again he, the self he wants to perpetuate, that comes indomitably alive.

It was inevitable that Unamuno should choose yet another aspect of his 'tragic sense' in his following novel, *Abel Sánchez*. It is perhaps the best-integrated of all the *nivolas*; Unamuno himself said that it was 'the most painful experiment he made, by plunging his scalpel into the worst tumor of our Spanish caste'. He was referring to the Spanish disease of envy, of which he himself was not free. Yet *Abel Sánchez* is not a social study except by inference; it is a modern version of the story of Cain and Abel.

Unamuno created two ordinary cultured Spaniards and endowed one, Abel Sánchez, with the gift to be popular, liked and successful, the other, Joaquín Monegro, with the gift to be intelligent, unattractive, over-sensitive and envious of the love he cannot win. The two grow up together, almost like brothers. From childhood onwards Joaquín feels hurt and mutinous when he sees how easily Abel attracts affection and applause. Abel becomes a fashionable painter, Joaquín a doctor profoundly dedicated to his profession. Joaquín falls in love with his cousin Helena, a shallow girl who dislikes his earnest intensity. She falls for Abel, who accepts her affection without any deeper feeling; if Joaquín suffers through their marriage it is not Abel's fault, as he and Helena are quick to point out. Joaquín, tortured by his frustrated love, his insufficiency and the other's effortless success, becomes obsessed with his love-hatred for Abel though he hates himself for it. His marriage with a good, simple, pious woman who is devoted to him brings no essential relief. He is too blinded by his craving for the unattainable and too self-centred to give her his love in return. When his rebellion against his own nature, which he had not chosen for himself, turns into revolt against the universe, his wife makes him seek the advice of a kind priest, although he has no faith in the Church. He asks the priest: 'What have I done that God made me like this, spiteful, envious and bad?' The answer that his will is free and he can be good is unacceptable to a doctor, who has seen people suffering helplessly because of a body and mind they cannot change. He is free only to be bad, he tells the priest. A friend suggests that such a festering hatred could only be dissolved by action, but this form of liberation is unthinkable to Joaquín; it would be murder. The other form of liberation would be his own death, the death of the personality which he hates but cannot even wish to change.

Abel, who is aware of his friend's preoccupation with the legend of Cain and blithely identifies himself with the good, guiltless biblical Abel, lends Joaquín Byron's *Cain*. The poem of the 'great denier' produces a violent revulsion from death and a tenuous belief in immortality in Joaquín. But he suffers new agonies of envy when his wife has a daughter, while Helena and Abel have a son such as he had longed for. Abel is not worthy of his son, just as he had proved by his facile love affairs that he is not worthy of Helena's love; he has no real affection for the boy and later makes him study medicine rather than letting him develop his bent for painting, because he is afraid and envious of future competition. When Joaquín discovers this, he concentrates his affection on Abel's son and neglects his own daughter. Yet when this daughter wishes to become a nun, he refuses his consent and influences her so that she finally marries young Abel, half from pity for her father's suffering. Joaquín's hopes for peace are again shattered when he finds that his and Abel's little grandson prefers the gayer, more playful grandfather who paints pictures for him. Abel is a sick man, he has a serious heart disease, but Joaquín knows himself to be incurably sick in his soul. In the end he tackles Abel and reproaches him with stealing all affection from him, deliberately, in the guise of kindness. When Abel insults him, Joaquín grasps him by the throat in desperate fury. Though he drops his hands immediately, the shock is enough to kill Abel.

Joaquín has turned himself into Cain, morally at least, as he had always feared. He lets himself sink into melancholy and physical illness from which no care and tenderness of his family can rescue him. In his last hour he makes his confession to all those he had loved. At first he accuses his destiny: 'What have I done to be like this? . . . Why was I born in a country full of hatred . . . for I have lived hating myself; here we all live hating ourselves.' But at the very end he accuses himself of his one real sin, that of not loving and not having wanted to love his wife. Through their love he might have found salvation. Even then he is true to himself and does not pretend that now, at the last moment, he feels love for her. He only feels a hopeless sorrow, and dies.

This spiritual, or psychopathological, case history is told through dialogue and extracts from Joaquín's 'Confessions', written for his daughter. Again there are no descriptions, only the bare bones of a human conflict. Abel, though drawn with far less sympathy than Joaquín, emerges as a definite individual, amiable, easy-going, smug, devoid of genuine pity, and therefore in one sense guilty of Joaquín's sufferings: guilty and yet not guilty, for Abel, too, did not choose to be what he was. On one level Unamuno makes this short novel a study of envy, from the type of envy which is a fundamentally noble obsession to the shoddy envy of the go-getter. On a deeper level he again poses the question which underlay *Niebla*, in a somewhat different version: Why must we live chained to a self which is not of our own choosing? Again, he offers no solution to the tragic conflict, only the vaguest hope of a possible salvation through compassionate love. As he took the side of his creature Augusto against himself in *Niebla*, he now takes the side of the rebel, the unhappy Cain, not so much against the fortunate, shallow Abel, but against his Creator. In a preface to the second edition of *Abel Sánchez* (1928) he says: 'In re-reading my *Abel Sánchez* . . . I have felt the greatness of my Joaquín Monegro's passion, and his moral superiority to all the Abels. The evil is not in Cain; it is in all the petty little Cains, and in all the petty little Abels.'

In my opinion, *Abel Sánchez* is much more successful than *Niebla* in the fusion between the religious or philosophical problem and the imaginative narration. As the author of one of the best studies on Unamuno, José Ferrater Mora, says in another context, Unamuno's personages appear scarcely 'realistic' to a literary critic, but they will never be less than real to a poet. This is at least true of his agonized heroes such as Joaquín, of those figures whom Unamuno began to call his 'agonists'.

He uses this phrase, and speaks of novels as poems, in his prologue to three short novels published in 1920 under the title of *Tres novelas ejemplares*. They are, he says, examples of life and reality; not of the 'everyday, crepuscular reality' caught in timid photographic descriptions, but of the 'intimate reality'. 'Every human man has within him the seven capital virtues and the seven capital vices, and with them he is capable of creating agonists of every sort'.

Of the three 'exemplary' stories, the best example of his creation of 'agonists' is the short novel *Nada menos que todo un hombre (Nothing if not a Man)*. At first sight, it is very different from Unamuno's other works. It is dramatic, indeed melodramatic, so much so that the dramatized version was very successful on the stage. The hero, Alejandro Gómez, seems the exact opposite of sensitive, overbred sufferers like Augusto or Joaquín. He is a rough man of action, a plebeian, self-made and of obscure origin. He has come back to Spain from America, where he made a fortune, with the conviction that nothing can resist his will, strength and money. His favourite saying is that he is 'nothing if not a man', a real man, and therefore the master of his own and other people's fate. He meets the reigning beauty of the small provincial town where he has made his new home, and at once decides to marry her. Julia, a proud and sensitive girl, is in distress because her father wants to force her into marriage with a wealthy brute, so as to get out of his dangerously pressing debts; two earlier engagements of hers had come to nothing because of the suitors' moral cowardice. Alejandro pays her father's debts and tells her that she must and shall marry him. His rocklike strength fascinates her against her will. She begins to love him without knowing what he really feels about her, and expects to gain his love after their marriage. Then her tragedy begins.

Alejandro shows not the slightest feeling for her and rejects her anxious questions as sentimental nonsense. She is his wife, that is enough. But Julia loves him too much to be content with her position as a prized property. She exhausts herself in vain attempts to change his hard, utilitarian attitude. Not even the birth of their first child, a son, affects his manner; 'he was always sure he would get what he wanted'. On the verge of hysteria, Julia begins to flirt with an amourous young Count so as to make her husband jealous, but the time-honoured trick fails. Things like a wife's faithlessness cannot happen to him, he says. After a nervous breakdown, Julia accepts the Count as her lover so that she can try to goad Alejandro into some sort of emotion, be it murderous fury. He tells her that she is mad, for 'his wife cannot do that to him—to him!' In any case, he is not willing to speak in the language of novels to her.

He confirms his self-assurance by letting Julia be certified as suffering from mental delusions, in the presence of the Count who is too much afraid of Alejandro to confirm her sanity. In the asylum, Julia fears to go mad in earnest and retracts her statement: of course she was deluded, the Count could never have been the lover of Alejandro's wife! Her husband accepts this as his due. But then he lets himself go for the first time and tells her that he loves her with his whole being, that he is 'more hers than she his'. On their return home, however, he withdraws behind his impassive mask and even bids Julia to forget his outbreak. To cap his victory he invites the Count to dinner and leaves him alone with Julia. When the Count speaks of the injustice done to her, Julia insists that she had been out of her senses. How could there ever have been any intimacy between them? The young man flees in terror from her. But the sequence of shocks has been too much for Julia. She collapses, and lingers for a while in delirious half-madness in which only her passion for her husband remains clear. Alejandro refuses to believe that his wife can die, that he cannot buy her life either by money or by offering himself as victim to a God of whom he had never thought before. His terrible, icy despair makes the dying woman happy, for now she knows that he loves her. With her last breath she begs him: 'Now tell me at last who you are.' He answers: 'Nothing but your man —what you've made me.' After her death he locks himself up with her body and shoots himself.

This short novel is an example of the deadly effect of a self-imposed rule of bleak reason, an example of the supremacy of passionate feeling and of the destroying force of such a feeling when it is turned inwards, robbed of its natural human outlets. Julia is unhappy, but the real tragedy is that of Alejandro, the 'tyrant out of timidity' (in Unamuno's definition elsewhere), the prisoner of his artificial personality and executioner of his own happiness. As long as he is proud of being 'nothing if not a man', he is less than human and doomed to terrifying loneliness. It takes the ultimate reality of death to transform Alejandro's tragic and yet ludicrous rationality into tragic sentiment.

In his prologue, Unamuno says (and this is one statement of his mystical brand of existentialism):

> Apart from what one is to God—if one is anything to God!—and apart from what one is to others and what one believes oneself to be, there is something else: what one wants to be. And this is, in one's inmost self, the creative force and true reality . . . God rewards or punishes one to be, for all eternity, what one had wanted to be.

The example I have just summarized shows a man punished in life by what he wanted to be to others, but it leaves it to the reader's imagination what Alejandro wanted to be within himself, underneath his armour. This reticence adds much to the poetic force of the story. The narrative could not be more terse and harsh, in language or structure; it has no trace of psycho-analytical probing or interior monologue, no adjectives to paint the physical shapes of the two protagonists—the agonists; there is no definition of Alejandro's agony. But the struggle and suffering are there, intensely alive.

Unamuno's next *nivola*, published in 1921, was, of course, another example of the spiritual conflict and fight of a human individual. The heroine of *La tía Tula (Aunt Tula)*, Gertrudis, is one of two beautiful sisters, a far stronger personality than the other. She is secretly in love with her sister's fiancé and discovers that he, too, loves her so much that he would prefer to break off his engagement. She forces him to go through with the marriage and imposes on herself the sacrifice of watching over its happiness. Her strong maternal yearnings find an outlet when her sister and Ramiro have children. The sister dies young. On her death-bed she asks Gertrudis to marry Ramiro rather than let the children have a stepmother: Gertrudis is their second mother in any case. But Gertrudis refuses Ramiro again, against her own instincts and despite his strong passion. In this self-punishing renunciation, pride—she does not wish to be a substitute, nor a 'remedy' for the man's sensual needs—is inextricably mixed with an ideal of purity. Against the wordly-wise and kind advice of her confessor she shuts herself up as though in a convent cell of her mind, in 'burning solitude', tortured by doubts about the value and meaning of her acts. Her profound piety does not help her; she is, though a devout and loyal Catholic, in her own way a heterodox who must work out her own salvation.

Ramiro feels betrayed and deserted by Gertrudis. As a challenge, and out of his immediate need, he seduces a servant girl and has a child by her. Gertrudis makes him marry his mistress, but stays at her post as the spiritual mother of the whole family, a peacemaker without inner peace. After the death of Ramiro and his second wife it is Gertrudis who keeps the family united and brings up two generations in mutual charity and understanding. Finally she dies 'in gentle agony', to live on as an ever-present inspiration for her 'children'. And yet, her last message to them is that they should 'think well, so that they would not have to repent of what they had done, and even less to repent of what they had left undone'. They must not be afraid of 'filth', for nobody can help a beloved being by trying to stay unsullied and remote.

Thus, despite its harmonious ending, this novel conveys a tragic sense of waste and loss, and tends to make the reader revolt against it. Unamuno considered that this tale had its roots in the spirit of 'his' Don Quixote, and in that of St. Theresa of Avila, the un-mystical mystic whom he revered. Read superficially, *La tía Tula* is the nearest to orthodox religion of all his works. Yet because Unamuno could not help being a questioner, the last message of Gertrudis calls the purpose of her whole life into question and unveils the unsolved doubt behind that saintly abnegation. There is a terrible hidden kinship between her and Alejandro Gómez.

The last of Unamuno's novels, *San Manuel, Bueno, mártir*, published in 1933 when he was nearly seventy, takes the problem up where *La Tía Tula* left it, carries it on, and back, to the central question of *The Tragic Sense of Life*, and so closes the circle. The amazing consistency of one who took delight in contradicting himself shows here most clearly: the final profession of faith is nothing but a poetic condensation of what he thought and wrote twenty years earlier. There is no softening of the edges, no old-age compromise in *San Manuel, Bueno, mártir*, only a deeper sadness, a more naked struggle. To speak in Unamuno's language: this story is his tragic sense of human life made flesh.

Story? There is no story of happenings. The narrator, Angela, an unmarried woman of good family, living in a beautiful mountain region of Galicia, in a village of poor peasants, records her memories of the parish priest Don Manuel Bueno who was her 'Spiritual Father' and is her abiding love. The Bishop is collecting material about him, for a memorandum which is to argue his beatification. Among the people he is called Saint Manuel Bueno; the shining goodness, humility and simplicity of his life continue to be inspiration and comfort to them in their drab existence. But since Angela's brother Lázaro died, she alone knows the priest's secret which made him truly a saint and a martyr, though not in a sense the ecclesiastic authorities could ever accept.

This was his secret as she records it: Don Manuel could not believe—or thought he could not believe—in the faith he was instilling in others; he wanted to believe with all his soul, was unable to deceive himself, and suffered the tortures of the damned for living a lie. It would have been a liberation to him to end this lie, but he knew that it was his cross to work as a priest, so that the poor people he loved should go on 'dreaming', protected by their faith from the devastating truth of death.

Angela, though Don Manuel's constant helper and companion since her early youth, had never guessed his agony; she had only seen his Christian deeds and felt his greatness. It was her brother, on his return from overseas where he had imbibed superficial anti-clerical ideas, who discovered it. At first Lázaro had accused Don Manuel of reactionary leanings and hypocrisy; later, after hearing a sermon, he had thought Don Manuel 'too intelligent to believe what he has to teach'. But after the death of his and Angela's mother he made friends with the priest and suddenly began to go to Mass and Communion, to his sister's great joy. Unexpectedly he told her the truth which shook her to the core. Don Manuel had convinced him of his duty to feign a faith he did not possess, for the sake of others, and had convinced him through his own example. 'Truth?' the priest had said, 'Truth may be something terrible, something unbearable and deadly. Simple people could not live on with it.' Lázaro had asked him why he was telling his secret to him, as though in confession. The priest had answered that it saved him from having to cry out in his torment before the others, when it was his task to 'make them happy, to let them dream that they are immortal, and not to kill them'. His only consolation was that he could give consolation to others.

The girl Angela, secure in her faith, spoke to Don Manuel almost like a confessor and asked him whether he did not believe in another life. He, who was ready to deceive others, would not answer her, but begged her to pray for him: 'We must live—and give life.' And: 'In the name of the people, Angelina, do you absolve me?' In maternal compassion, and at the same time with a mystic assurance, she gave him the absolution he asked for.

Lázaro began to change under the impact of Don Manuel's agonized goodness and to mould himself after his pattern. He learnt that the priest had to resist a longing to drown himself in the peaceful lake: 'Let's go on killing ourselves in our work and our people, so that the people can go on dreaming their life as the lake dreams the sky.' Lázaro even accepted the priest's opinion that it was better not to destroy people's superstitions: 'Better they believe everything than nothing.' While he shouldered the burden of hiding his unbelief, in order to help his friend and others, Angela found her Catholic faith strengthened by the doubt and suffering of Don Manuel, because it seemed a true saint's martyrdom to her.

Worn out in body and soul, the priest prepared for his death. First he took leave of the only two beings who knew him: 'Never to see each other again, for this dream of life has come to its end . . . You, Angela, go on praying that all sinners may dream of a resurrection of the flesh and life everlasting, till they die . . .'

Don Manuel turned his death into a last act of self-denial and of consolation for his 'poor people'. From his armchair, below the altar, he told them to live in peace until they would meet again among the stars, in a heavenly village. Then he blessed them, prayed with them, and finally spoke the Credo in which he could not believe. Immediately after his death the people went in search of relics of their saint. Lázaro died soon after. One of the last things he told his sister was that Don Manuel had suspected that all the greatest among the Saints of the Church had died without believing in an after-life. Lázaro did not mind dying, but regretted that with him 'another bit of Don Manuel would die'; though some of him would live on in Angela 'until one day we shall all die, even the dead'.

In her memoirs, written many years later, Angela puts all this down, trying to puzzle out the meaning. She has at long last understood why Don Manuel had not hidden his secret from Lázaro: nothing but 'his truth' could have converted her brother to Don Manuel's 'most holy game'. He 'gained him for the cause of life by the truth of death'. She still thinks that the priest and her brother only believed themselves to be disbelievers, through a mysterious act of God, and would see more clearly after their transition. But at the very end, in the last sentence, she too asks: 'And I, do I believe?'

In a bitter little epilogue Unamuno contends that, even had his Don Manuel and his Lázaro revealed their unbelief to 'the people', those simple villagers would have neither understood nor believed them because works and conduct were the only valid confession in their eyes. 'The people neither know what a sort of thing faith is, nor do they care much about it.'

This was written in Salamanca in 1930, nearly three years before the novel was published, and a few months after Unamuno's return from exile. There is another set of apparent contradictions in this fact. Since 1914, when he was relieved from his rectorship because of his bitter attacks against the system of the Spanish monarchy and against a nominal democracy which only corrupted the people, he had never ceased to fight against all that is commonly called reaction, not least against a political clergy that threatened to destroy all true religious feeling. The workers of Salamanca had come out in strike when they heard of his dismissal. At the beginning of the twenties, when General Miguel Primo de Rivera established his benevolent military dictatorship to save the throne, Unamuno had become so vehement in his denunciation of dictatorial methods that he was banished to Fuerteventura in the Canary Islands. From there he had fled to France, to live in exile first in Paris, then in Hendaye, in the Basque country of France where he could feel close to his native soil; he had become a symbol of the spiritual fight for freedom among the intellectuals of the world. After the fall of the dictatorship, in February 1930, Unamuno had returned to his country as a triumphant forerunner of the new Spain, and in his first great speeches he had sounded the tocsin for King Alfonso's rule. It was he who gave the inaugural address at Salamanca University the next year, re-instated as Rector, no longer in the name of the King but in the name of 'Her Imperial and Catholic Majesty, Spain'. He went to the Constituent Cortes of the Republic as a deputy of the Republican bloc, though not as the member of any party. And yet–this was the apparent contradiction to which I referred–the first great work he wrote after his return to Spain could be taken, and often was taken, as his final rejection of all social changes that could lead to a destruction of the people's unquestioning traditional faith. Simultaneously, however, the new generation and those who shared Unamuno's dislike for the political activities of the clergy and their 'theology', read *San Manuel, Bueno, mártir* as though it were a final anti-clerical indictment; an indictment not against the tortured priest who embodied a lie out of love for the people, but against the many others who tried to keep the Spanish villages submerged in dark ignorance because it guaranteed the power of their organisation.

It has often been said, by Unamuno himself and by others, that he was always fighting in his own mind the chronic civil war of Spain because the 'two Spains' were so powerfully alive in him that he belonged to neither and to both. The final poetic realisation of this tragic split, *San Manuel, Bueno, mártir*, marks the beginning of a new phase in Unamuno's mental civil war. Although it re-stated what he had felt and expressed since 1898, the atmosphere in which it was written, and even more that in which it was published, gave it a different resonance. The imaginary parish of Don Manuel still had its counterparts in reality, in miserably poor villages all over Spain, but those villages were beginning to suffer an irrevocable change. They were indeed suffering it: the intrusion of new technical methods and material needs, slow and fitful as it was, brought them vague but passionate hopes and disappointments. Many whose Catholic faith had never been inspired by spiritual longings, as Unamuno had seen so clearly, lapsed into complete indifference; others embraced a new non-religious creed with violent fervour and turned with equal violence against the Church by whom they felt cheated; the simple souls who remained unaffected by doubt were few. In the other camp, most defenders of the Catholic tradition of Spain had nothing but their authoritarian doctrine to set against the new mass movements. Unamuno watched both trends with despair. And it was this despair, superimposed on his 'tragic sense', which he poured into *San Manuel, Bueno, mártir*. At a juncture when the greater part of Spaniards were carried away by optimism at the rise of the Republic, the old thinker who had helped to prepare their minds for the Republic began his last, great, lonely battle for the spiritual Spain he had preached. It was, inevitably, a battle against both sides, and it lasted till his death during the Civil War.

In an article for the newspaper *Ahora*, written in 1933, Unamuno explained, against his critics, why he had not followed his Don Manuel's example of self-abnegation and why he had confessed his disbelief. First of all he repeated his opinion that 'simple souls' cannot be hurt in their faith even if they are told that they had been deceived. They cannot believe it. Secondly he confirmed that he thought a definite religious faith—even 'a deceit'—the best state for 'infantile souls'. But then he went on to say drily that, unfortunately, communities did not consist of simple souls alone and that in Spain 'the infantile unconsciousness of the people produced in the end worse damage than an intimate, tragic anxiety'. They went from one opiate to another, from a religion they had not really felt to a materialistic creed that could give them a 'vital illusion'. A harsh, bitter awareness of the insoluble human problem, however, saves the inner life. 'The truth will set you free.'

Yet the years of the Spanish Republic, from 1931 to 1936, were filled with conflicts on another plane than the spiritual. Unamuno grew more isolated, disappointed and embittered, despite the public and international honours heaped on him. After the dissolution of the Constituent Cortes he withdrew from the active political life where he had never felt at home, because he was too clearly conscious of good and bad on both sides to fit into a pattern. Guillermo de Torre, a distinguished Spanish critic in exile (whose essay *The Agony of Unamuno* supplies otherwise hardly accessible material on Unamuno's end) says that the old man's last lecture in the Ateneo of Madrid in 1933 'struck many of us as the swan song of liberalism'. From his citadel of Salamanca, Unamuno wrote article after article of acute, often unpopular and often cantankerous criticism, directed against every sort of slogan, Right or Left, against Marxism, against urban mass movements, and against the new generation of europeanisers. More vehemently than ever he extolled the 'Spanishness' of Spain and her mission to conquer a world for 'his' Don Quixote and the spirit of the Spanish mystics, though not for the Spanish Inquisitors and theologians. He gave free rein to his many personal prejudices, perhaps driven by a profound disillusionment at his isolation which honours such as his rectorship for life, and the Freedom of the Republic as 'honorary citizen', could not conceal.

Once more, in 1934, he wrote a *nivola*, but this time in dramatic form, an 'old comedy renewed' on the myth of Don Juan which is as Spanish as Don Quixote. He called it *Brother Juan or The World is a Stage*; and it is as radically opposed to Shaw's treatment of the myth of Don Juan in *Man and Superman* as Unamuno's tragic sense of life is to Shaw's life force. There his Brother Juan asks: 'Does Don Miguel de Unamuno exist? Is it not all a misty dream?' The mist was thickening fast.

On July 17th, 1936, the Spanish Civil War broke out. Salamanca was for a long time the headquarters of General Franco's military and civil administration. At first Unamuno declared himself in favour of the rebels, not because he shared the ideas of the fascists among them, but because he hoped that the movement would save Spain from the mass rule which was his nightmare, and revive the 'living tradition'. Very little is known about his last valiant attack on those in power, as soon as he had realised that they had nothing whatever to do with the aspirations of his own spirit. At the inauguration of the university year, on October 12th, 1936, Unamuno, the Rector, rose to speak against the cult of violence embodied in General Millán Astray, the man who had invented the battle cry 'Long live Death!' and who now, in the Ceremonial Hall, had perorated against the 'bad Spaniards' on the other side. When Unamuno declared that there were patriots and anti-patriots in both camps and that a crippled Spain would be a negative creation, he was shouted down, and someone cried: *Muera la inteligencia!*—'Death to the Intelligentsia'. Or perhaps it should be translated as: 'Death to Intelligence!'

Unamuno was relieved of his post at once. Whether sterner measures were contemplated is not certain. He stayed in his house, as though under arrest, guarded by police. Guillermo de Torre quotes reports of a Dutch journalist to whom Unamuno spoke shortly before his death; he had come to believe that the Nationalists were 'the enemies of all that stands for the spirit in this world'. We do not know more about his last agony of the mind. Miguel de Unamuno died in the night of New Year's Eve, 1936. There are differences of opinion on whether the cerebral stroke killed him on the last day of the old or on the first day of the new year.

The rest is not silence; his work will live on. I have bypassed two of Unamuno's greatest books, *Vida de Don Quijote y Sancho* which epitomizes his thoughts on the Spanish spiritual tradition, and *La agonía del cristianismo* which contains his most complete search into the problems of Christianity and Catholicism. I have neglected his ideas on men and women—on the 'sisterly' compassionate love he looked for in women—and on celibacy which he abhorred and called 'monkish solitary sensuality'. It would be possible to place him in the stream of modern philosophical thought, among the anti-rationalists and vitalists. It would be tempting to portray the man: his wisdom and vanity; his endless perambulations in the countryside when he talked to friends, students and strangers, always in monologues, always in need of an audience; his whimsies, as for instance the paper birds he fabricated and gave to his friends; his puckish publicity tricks, and all the qualities in which he was the most Spanish of Spaniards. But the list is endless. To everything one says about Unamuno, as to everything he said, one could find a passage in his works which contradicts it, and for every theory one could find passages in support.

And in the end it is always the complete unity of the man and his work, the man and his life, which emerges with overwhelming force. Through his failures and successes, mistakes and creative acts, through his insistence on the life-giving doubt, he achieved what he wanted to achieve: there is no thinking Spaniard who has not, wittingly or unwittingly, felt the influence of Miguel de Unamuno's goading, stimulating, irritating and humbling thought. If in the present generation his agony and incurable inner schism touch us all, he has also left us a legacy of moral courage and integrity. A thinker who teaches how to turn conflict, contradiction and despair into a source of strength has something to give to men of this age.

BIOGRAPHICAL NOTES

Miguel de Unamuno y Jugo born Bilbao, 20th April 1864.
Secondary education at Instituto Vizcaino, Bilbao, 1875-1879.
University of Madrid 1880-1884, Philosophy and Ancient Languages, Ph. D.
1884-1891 resident in Bilbao; marriage, private tutoring, literary work.
1891 appointed Professor of Greek, Salamanca University.
1901 appointed Rector of Salamanca University until relieved of post for political reasons in 1914.
1924 deported to Fuerteventura, Canary Islands, because of political attacks on Spanish monarchy and the military dictatorship of General Primo de Rivera. Flight to France, June 1924.
1924-1930 exile in France, first in Paris, then in Hendaye.
1930 returned to Spain (Salamanca) after the fall of the dictatorship.
1931 re-elected Rector of Salamanca University.
1931-1933 Deputy to the Constituent Cortes of the new Republic, as member of Republican bloc, but not of any specific party.
1934 declared Rector of Salamanca University for his lifetime.
1936 on outbreak of Nationalist Revolution first declared himself in its favour, later took public stand against it at inauguration of University year at Salamanca. Again removed from rectorship by Nationalist authorities and confined to his house until his death.
Died 31st December, 1936.

UNAMUNO'S MOST IMPORTANT WORKS

As no complete critical edition exists of Unamuno's works, any bibliography is bound to be faulty. The most notable gaps are the lack of a complete collection of the articles and essays scattered over a great number of periodicals, of an edition of his theatrical work, and of a separate edition of his poetry. Many of his poems are interspersed among essays and travel sketches.

Of Unamuno's vast correspondence little has been published. Notable are his letters to Leopoldo Alas ('Clarín') contained in *Epistolario a Clarín*, Madrid, 1941, and thirty-six letters to Jiménez Ilundain, first published and introduced in *El drama religioso de Unamuno* by Hernán Benitez, Buenos Aires, 1949.

The following list is a guide to the most important works, and includes mention of translations into English.

En torno al casticismo, Madrid, 1895.

Paz en la guerra, Madrid, 1897.

Tres ensayos (*Adentro!, La Ideocracia, La fé*), Madrid, 1900.

Amor y pedagogía, Barcelona, 1902.

Vida de Don Quijote y Sancho, Madrid, 1905.

(*The Life of Don Quixote and Sancho*, trans. H. P. Earle, London and New York, 1927.)

Poesías, Madrid, 1907.

Recuerdos de niñez y de mocedad, Madrid, 1908.

Rosario de sonetos líricos, Madrid, 1910.

Contra esto y aquello, Madrid, 1912.

Del sentimiento trágico de la vida en los hombres y en los pueblos, Madrid, 1913.

(*The Tragic Sense of Life in Men and in Peoples*, trans. J. E. C. Flitch, intro. by Salvador de Madariaga, London and New York, 1921.)

Niebla (*Nivola*), Madrid, 1914.

(*Mist, a tragicomic novel*, trans. W. Fite, New York, 1928.)

Ensayos, 7 vols., Madrid, 1916, 1917, 1918 (collected essays).

Tres novelas ejemplares y un prólogo, Madrid, 1920.

(*Three Exemplary Novels and a Prologue*, trans. A. Flores, New York, 1930.)

Abel Sánchez, Madrid, 1921.

La tía Tula, Madrid, 1921.

Como se hace una novela, Buenos Aires, 1927. (This was first published in French, *Comment se fait un roman*, trans. Jean Cassou, Paris, 1926.)

Romencero del destierro, Buenos Aires, 1928.
La agonía del cristianismo, Madrid, 1931. (This was first published in French, *L'agonie du christianisme*, trans. Jean Cassou, Paris, 1926.)
(*The Agony of Christianity*, trans. P. Loving, New York, 1928.)
San Manuel, Bueno, mártir y tres historias más, Madrid, 1933.
El hermano Juan o el mundo es teatro, Madrid, 1934.

The following were published posthumously:
La ciudad de Henoc, Mexico, 1941 (articles of 1933).
Cuenca iberica, Mexico, 1943 (articles of 1932-1933).